A Nightmare on Horseback

A Nightmare on Horseback

Poems by

Robert Cooperman

© 2022 Robert Cooperman. All rights reserved.
This material may not be reproduced in any form, published,
reprinted, recorded, performed, broadcast,
rewritten or redistributed without
the explicit permission of Robert Cooperman.
All such actions are strictly prohibited by law.

Cover design by Shay Culligan
Cover image by Pablo Hkhotjecsgy

ISBN: 978-1-63980-168-8

Kelsay Books
502 South 1040 East, A-119
American Fork, Utah 84003
Kelsaybooks.com

For Skip Westcott

And as Always, for Beth

Acknowledgments

The following poems have either appeared or are forthcoming, some in earlier form, in the journals listed below:

Concho River Review: "Gone-Nose Watches Over John Sprockett and Remembers His Banishment from His Tribe," "The Raid on Lawrence, Kansas, William Quantrill," "John Sprockett Keeps Watch As Quantrill's Raiders Strip B.J. Pettibone's Store"

Horror Sleazy Trash: "John Sprockett Buys a Mount for Sylvia Williams"

Misfit Magazine: "Riding Farther into Kansas, John Sprockett Beds Down for the Night," "Camping by a Creek, John Sprockett Has an Unexpected Visitor," "Gone-Nose and John Sprockett Battle a Bear"

Pure Slush: "Ezekiel Smith, on Seeing John Sprockett in the Camp of Captain William Quantrill"

Contents

I—Unexpected Visitors

Riding West from the Shoot-Out, John Sprockett Mourns His Loved Ones	17
Riding Farther into Kansas, John Sprockett Beds Down for the Night	19
Camping by a Creek, John Sprockett Has an Unexpected Visitor: Kansas	21
Gone-Nose and John Sprockett Battle a Bear	23
Gone-Nose Watches Over John Sprockett	24
John Sprockett, after Being Mauled by a Grizzly	26
John Sprockett Begins to Heal	27
Gone-Nose and John Sprockett Have Visitors	29
John Sprockett Reflects on the Man He Shot	31
William Quantrill, After Meeting Young John Sprockett and Gone-Nose	33

II—The Demon-Riders

Gone-Nose, at the Prospect of Him and John Sprockett Riding with Quantrill's Raiders	37
Daniel Cruikshank, One of Quantrill's Raiders, Eyes John Sprockett and Gone-Nose with Suspicion	39
Ezekiel Smith, on Seeing John Sprockett in the Camp of Captain William Quantrill	41
Mrs. Lydia Watson, Southern Sympathizer	43
Frank James Explains One Source of Quantrill's Success to New Recruit, John Sprockett	44
John Sprockett Observes the Drawn Battle Lines	45
John Sprockett Thinks about the Kansas City Jail Incident	47

After His First Foray with Quantrill's Raiders,
   John Sprockett Considers His Situation   48
Gone-Nose, after the Raid on a Unionist Farm   49
Gone-Nose, after the Raid on the Unionist
   Farm, II   50

III—The Hell Road to Lawrence

On the Way to Lawrence, John Sprockett
   Ponders Slavery   55
Riding to Lawrence, John Sprockett Remembers
   His Beloved Sarah   56
John Sprockett Remembers His Stepfather,
   the Reverend Jeremiah Sprockett   57
William Quantrill, on the Road to Lawrence,
   Kansas, Inspects the Perdee Farm   59
Martin Rice, after Refusing to Help Provision
   William Quantrill's Raider's   61
Benjamin Potter Hears of William Quantrill's
   Treatment of Martin Rice   63
Benjamin Potter, Southern Sympathizer, Faces
   Execution   64
Martin Rice, at the Execution of Benjamin Potter   66
John Sprockett Looks Behind, As Quantrill's
   Raiders Ride for Lawrence   68
Gone-Nose Contemplates the Raid on Lawrence   69
Millie Spangler, Ten-Years-Old, Spots John
   Sprockett among Quantrill's Raiders   70
John Sprockett Listens to William Quantrill's
   Speech Before the Raid on Lawrence   71
John Sprockett and Quantrill's Raiders Ride
   Deeper into Kansas   72

Stephen J. Wilson, Sixteen, Clerk at B.J. Pettibone's Dry Goods, Gardner, Kansas	73
John Sprockett Keeps Watch As Quantrill's Raiders Strip B.J. Pettibone's Store	74
B.J. Pettibone Taken Hostage	75
John Sprockett and the No Longer Useful Guides	77
Isaiah Templeton, Forced To Guide Quantrill's Raiders	79
Outside Lawrence, Kansas: Gone-Nose Leaves Quantrill's Raiders	81
John Sprockett Watches Gone-Nose Leave Quantrill's Camp	83
Before the Raid on Lawrence, Quantrill Wakes to Find His Favorite Mount Gone	84
John Sprockett Hears William Quantrill's Speech before the Raid on Lawrence	86

IV—The Raid

Mrs. Millie Holcomb Witnesses the Shooting of Her Husband and Son	89
Abraham Jones, Hired Hand on the Holcomb Farm	90
The Raid on Lawrence, Kansas: William Quantrill	92
Sally McWhorter, School Teacher, Faces Down One of Quantrill's Raiders	94
Christopher McPherson, Twelve-Year-Old Schoolboy	96
Big Bob Tolliver	97
John Sprockett Goes His Own Way	98
Hattie Morris, Ten-Years-Old, as Quantrill's Raiders Return from the Raid on Lawrence	100

V—Traveling Companions

Leaving Quantrill's Raiders, John Sprockett Comes Upon a Traveling Companion	105
John Sprockett and Sylvia Williams Ride West	107
John Sprockett Continues Telling His Life Story to Sylvia Williams	109
Sylvia Williams Rides behind John Sprockett	111
John Sprockett Tries to Explain Why He Participated in the Raid on Lawrence	113
Sylvia Williams, after John Sprockett Has Told His Story	115
John Sprockett Begins to Teach Sylvia Williams How to Read and Write	117
John Sprockett Helps Buy a Mount for Sylvia Williams: September 1863	118
Sylvia Williams Saves John Sprockett from Hanging	120
Ellis Townshend, Mayor of Chatham	122
John Sprockett Has a Nightmare	123
At the Town of Quarry, Colorado Territory, Sylvia Williams Parts Company with John Sprockett	124
John Sprockett Bids Farewell to Sylvia Williams	126

I—Unexpected Visitors

Riding West from the Shoot-Out, John Sprockett Mourns His Loved Ones

I'm cursed, bringing death
to them I care more about
than sunrise: Sarah, the girl
I loved like a lifetime
of Christmas mornings;
she died squeezing our child
into the world, when we ran off
from her Pa and mine,
both of them hating me
like Judas and King Herod
rolled together into one
ball of evil.

And when my preacher step-Pa
killed Ma—frothing with knowing
I wasn't his—I avenged her hard,
though looking back
to when I was a growing lad,
I should've just let him beat me
every time he was took by
the demon of jealousy,
if it would've kept Ma alive.

Now, Miz Wilton, the kind lady
who took me and Neddie in,
on the run from that posse
that gunned her like a mad dog;
they were gleeful as hounds
with juicy bones to hang us,
those boys in the pay
of Sarah's rich, grief-mad Pa.

Last, Neddie, my little brother,
.45-scythed by the banker's son,
that grinning rat not caring
who he shot, long as it hurt me.
Neddie should've stayed in Turpin,
safe as a pokey carriage horse,
but he'd not let me ride away alone.

I blasted those shoot-first bastards
with the repeater I took
off the banker's son-of-a-bitch spawn,
left them to rot in the sleet
of this Kansas winter.
I buried Miz Wilton and Neddie,
said fitting poems over their graves,
but not even Mr. Shakespeare
can bring them back.

There's a hole in my heart
long and wide as a railroad line.
I fear it's turned me into something
even I'm afraid of, while I ride
as far from folks and their meanness
as I can, so I don't take vengeance
on the whole territory,
shoot, on the whole damn country.

Riding Farther into Kansas, John Sprockett Beds Down for the Night

Maybe a month ago
that I had it out with that posse.
I've not seen a soul since,
not even the tribes,
though they're surely lurking
behind a rise or over a hill,
keeping downwind,
so my mount can't sniff them
and give me fair warning.

Maybe word's gone round
I'm not to be trifled with:
a devil who might murder
the whole world, even now
that I've avenged Ma, Neddie,
my darling Sarah, and Miz Wilton:
her just getting in the way
of the mayhem and deviltry
that scents me out like wolves.

Bad as I am, that posse was worse,
killing Neddie and Miz Wilton
for the fun of dropping two lambs
after their liquor ran out:
meaner than just woke grizzlies.

Last I heard, the country's in the midst
of a war that'll tear us all apart,
and I'll have to fight men
I once called friends. At least
I've no kin left to get murdered.

After Sarah and me ran off,
she died in that rain-rotting barn,
trying to bring our baby
into this world harder than iron-drought
prairie summer ground.

I wish we'd never met,
never fell in love. She'd be alive
and I'd be Pa's drudge—but worth it
if Sarah was still in the world—
'stead of me being Pa's murderer.

Time to camp for the night.
Past time to fret over
what or who might be drawn
to the fire I've tickled
into dancing like Kiowa
about to go on the warpath.

I'm too hungry to care.
Shoot, I'd welcome savages:
If they don't kill you outright,
they feel obliged to offer hospitality.

Camping by a Creek, John Sprockett
Has an Unexpected Visitor: Kansas

I'd ate up the jerky and flitch
I took off the posse I turned
into bloody rags, with that Spencer
repeating rifle I separated from
the banker's son I sent to Hell,
for trying to kill me and for
murdering Neddie and Miz Wilton.

Still, those varmints' deaths
weigh on me; I'm torn between
riding to the Rockies, to live alone
and lonesome-away from folks
I could harm in the blink of an eye,
or now that war rages, head Back East
and along the Missouri border,
I might fight for one side or the other:
an excuse for the murder
that rises out of me
like those sulphur fountains
mountain men talk about,
in the Yellowstone.

For now I snare a jack rabbit
and roast it over the fire I tickled
with tinder and the deadfall
of cottonwoods leaning over the creek,
their branches cackling like the witches
in Mr. Shakespeare's *Macbeth*.
Then I'll bed down for the night,
sleep a mixed blessing of dark nothing
or maybe lightning-lit dreams of the men
I've killed and of my gone-to-heaven
dear ones.

But I'm woke by my mount's panic-shrieks,
frantic to free itself of its hobbles.
I hear the snuffling of something big.
If I'm lucky, it'll move on, or maybe
I'll get the death I deserve from the grizzly
I can scent like a row of latrines.

I edge my hunting blade out, and my .44—
the repeater useless at this close range—
and pray to the demon that watches
over me to make this monster find me
too scrawny for even a meager meal.

Gone-Nose and John Sprockett Battle a Bear

I been tracking that bear for days
when it snuffled around a white man's camp,
him pretending to be dead, hoping the beast
might amble off: the white most likely
shitting himself; then rage and blood:
The bear raking his face, him screaming,
stabbing, the beast roaring, him firing.

Somehow, I leaped onto the grizzled god,
my knife plunging into its hump and sides,
the white stabbing from below,
emptying his sidearm into the monster,
then twisting free and slashing, the beast
flailing with claws big as cooking pots,
its fangs longer than hunting knives.

Then, just a heap and half the man's face
ripped almost to the bone, bleeding
like a bison's pierced heart. I found herbs
and spider webs for a poultice he screamed
to feel against his face; I mixed a sleep potion
and when he was finally breathing quiet,
I set about the butchering, drying strips
by the fire, feasting on the good, rich liver.

The women of his tribe won't ever
look at him with longing again;
like the squaws of mine spat and hissed
at my nose-stump: punishment
for lying with a kinsman's wife.
They prodded me from our camp,
their lance-jabs shouting,

"Show your ruined face here again,
and we'll slice off your root!"

Gone-Nose Watches Over John Sprockett

The white sleeps, from the roots
I mixed with water and fed him
after we killed the monster-bear
that ruined his face, its claws bigger
than the rakes whites scrape off weeds
that choke their woman-crops.

Children will cry at the sight of him,
women, the ones he will have to pay,
will squeeze shut their eyes and shake,
until he is finished. Better if he lives alone,
like me, after my kinsman caught me
with his wife, her appetite for men
great as a bear's for food before the winter sleep.

She knew Badger Eyes would find us,
and wanted two almost-brothers
to fight for her, the mating more exciting
for her, if one kills the other.

"Finish him!" she hissed
when Badger Eyes rammed his musket stock
into my face, my nose a bloody stump.
"He took me without permission," she lied,
while I bled, everything spinning
like those waterspout clouds.
Instead, he commanded me
to live alone, like that great bear
the white and I fought off.

When the white wakes,
maybe he'll finish himself, or beg me to,
or become as monstrous as his face:
a curse to everyone who comes near him,
to anyone who stares in silent horror,
as if at a demon Wendigo,
at what's left of him.

By comparison, my splattered stump
is as handsome as the warriors
that stories are told of, to give girls
coming into womanhood dreams
of being taken and caressed afterwards
by those the gods bless.

John Sprockett, after Being Mauled by a Grizzly

Lord, it hurts! If not for this Pawnee
feeding me something to help me sleep,
I'd have killed myself, still might,
knowing what my face must look like,
all ripped to rags by that bear, meaner than Pa,
when he'd shout a hell-bound sermon,
or when Ma's dinners weren't to table
the instant he tromped in. Lord, I hated him,
made him pay for sending Ma where—
as she'd quote her beloved Mr. Shakespeare—
she'll have no more fear of the sun's heat,
nor of winter's raging cold and snows.

That grizzly was Pa's vengeance
from beyond the shallow grave I put him in,
and for dispatching the posse that came for me:
I woke in my camp to that monster's hell-breath:
his claws curious, then ripping, while I screamed
and slashed his belly, and that Pawnee appeared
out of nowhere, us two finally killing that beast.

Then everything went black, though I'll come to
in a world of pain 'til that Pawnee feeds me
more of that something that makes me sleep.
This ain't no way to live and expect
to see grandkids riding my knees
like a litter of rambunctious wolf cubs.

I 'spect, with the War bubbling like sulphur lakes,
I'll die in a hailstorm of bullets or a volley
of cannon fire loud as the trumpets of Hell:
'less I end this nightmare of being me.

John Sprockett Begins to Heal

The pain's a dull throb, not the agony
of scraping claws it was; still, I fear
to look into the creek and see
what that monster did to my face:
not that I was a feast for the eyes,
'cept to poor Sarah, who's in Heaven.

I'd be dead too, if not for this Pawnee,
Gone-Nose, mending me up,
his nose smashed to a stub
by a kinsman's musket stock:
the feller catching him with his wife.

I shudder to think half my face is a skull;
still, part of me's itching to see
how bad it is, so after maybe
five minutes, maybe an hour,
of squeezed shut eyes,
I stare into the stream.

Sweat's pouring off me
like I'd run and run from hostiles.
I fumble for my sidearm,
but Gone-Nose grabs it.
I ain't ever begged before,
but plead for my iron back,
or for him to be merciful
and shoot me himself.

'Stead, he points to riders
closing fast, hands me my .44.
Strange, a moment ago,

I was desperate to end
my miserable life; now,
we're in danger,
fighting's the only choice.

We wait for them to close on us,
or take one look at me and slap leather
like all the hounds of Hell are baring fangs.
The War's come to Kansas,
a need for raging men like me.

Gone-Nose and John Sprockett Have Visitors

I've grown to like the white I named "Skull."
Even if he can barely speak my tongue,
his presence keeps the silence at bay
as a roaring fire makes wolf packs
back away in the terror of night.

When I came upon him, being savaged
by the bear I'd been tracking for days,
we killed the beast. I gentled poultices
onto his ripped face, chanted spells,
and fed him a mash of roots, berries,
and leaves to help him sleep without pain.

Now, a band of white riders approaches,
so instead of letting Skull shoot himself—
as he'd tried, when he beheld his ruined face—
I point to those men riding like devil-winds:
chasing runaway slaves or fleeing a ghost-
Wendigo even more ferocious than the bear.

Five horse lengths away, they rein in,
their mounts snorting like a pig I once stole
from a white farmer. One of them laughs
and points at Skull's face. He raises his gun
and shoots the man, then mutters to the leader,
who nods and smiles, as much as a man
can smile while staring into the face of death.

The riders dismount, bury the dead man
without grumbling or shooting us,
and make camp. One of them speaks to Skull
in a manner that tells me they know each other.
Part of me wants to wait for nightfall,

and quietly steal a horse before they play with me
like wolf cubs taught to toy with a mouse
before killing it; but more, I want to stay
and see what will happen next.

John Sprockett Reflects on the Man He Shot

Sad to say, it gets easier
to send men to Heaven or Hell.
True, I didn't hesitate with Pa,
but that was revenge. Nor did I
waste a tear on that posse:
they'd have exalted me
from a cottonwood, had not
that Spenser gave me an edge.

This feller's the first I've killed
just for laughing at my wreck of a face,
though I doubt he'll be the last.
I should've given him a chance to apologize,
but rage blinded me; my .44 splattered him.
The leader of the men he rode with—
Captain Quantrill—allowed:

"Caleb wasn't ever going to live a long,
happy life, with his big, dumb mouth.
We're a band," he went on, "fighting
for our sacred Confederacy; you
and your redskin pal are free to join us,"
dangling an unspoken noose of,

"If you don't . . ."

"Sir, your crusade is ours,"
I may be but seventeen, but no fool,
though I fear bodies will pile up
by my hand, for less and less cause:
each corpse a bear trap mangling me
down to Hell.

Besides, looking at and talking to
some of these dust-covered riders,
I see boys I grew up with in Turpin;
maybe we weren't fast friends,
but in times like these, you got
to stick to the ones you know.

William Quantrill, After Meeting Young John Sprockett and Gone-Nose

That Sprockett's a born killer;
he'll replace Caleb: that stupid
son of a whore laughing
at the boy's bear-ruined face;
a shame: the untouched part's
pleasing as John Wilkes Booth.
It'll be a pleasure to watch
the kid take vengeance
against Federal bands attacking
farms and towns abiding by
our Constitution-sacred,
slave-holding laws.
And didn't Jesus warn,

"Slaves, obey your masters"?

When we came across him
and his equally none-too-pleasant-
looking Pawnee pard, Caleb laughed
at the kid's misfortune and got
what he deserved. Rather than us
putting more holes into them two
than in a mouse-nibbled cheese wheel,
I set men to burying that idjit,
and proposed to Sprockett and the 'skin—
who glared, probably not knowing a word—
that they join us in righteous retribution.

Sprockett's got so much rage in him,
he could murder all of Abolitionist Kansas;
I doubt he's squeamish about shooting women
and kids, like some fellers are.

But this is war, and Federals slaughter
every good Sesech they come across:
and that includes mee-maws, nursing mothers,
pig-tailed gals in calico frocks, and lads
with straw-colored cowlicks and more
freckles than seeds in strawberries.

And that ain't even mentioning
the wives and sisters of some of the boys
I ride with that were blown up
in that Kansas City jail fire,
too convenient to call it an accident.

Only fair we show no mercy, too,
though some might accuse that'll lead
to universal butchery. So be it,
long as we come out on top!

II—The Demon-Riders

Gone-Nose, at the Prospect of Him and John Sprockett Riding with Quantrill's Raiders

The whites' speech?
The screeching of a crow
to everyone but a shaman,
not the language of real men,
but they need Skull and me
to raid their enemy's settlements,
after Skull killed one their warriors,
for laughing at the gullies and ravines
that grizzly tore down Skull's face.

Lucky the bear missed his eyes,
before the two of us plunged knives in,
over and over, until the god's spirit
returned to the Land of Good Hunting,
to forage and fuck for eternity.

My face disfigured by a kinsman as well,
my rage spurts like hot fountains,
so I welcome the taking of white scalps,
though the ones I'll help will claim the land
my tribe owns, once they drive
their enemies under the soil.

If I ride with them long enough,
I'll learn their weaknesses and send them
to the Land of Cold Shadows: the shit-
stinking swamp they sprang from.
Or I could just wait until darkness,
and silent as rising mist,

slit their throats: to rid us
of them all, and maybe win back
my place with my tribe, my kinsman
gratefully ceding me his woman,
for my feats of bravery.

Daniel Cruikshank, One of Quantrill's Raiders, Eyes John Sprockett and Gone-Nose with Suspicion

I ain't beheld two uglier specimens
in all my days, which, I admit, ain't
that long, being but seventeen myself,
Sprockett's age, but 'cause of his grizzly
ripped face, he looks older'n Bobby Lee.

He cradles that Spencer repeating rifle
like it's a gold nugget big as a bison skull.
I bet he stole it, only fair if I relieve him of it,
to protect Missouri from Abolitionist armies.

Sprockett don't talk much; the Injun not at all,
and I'd not trust either far as I could toss
a cottonwood, 'specially after Sprockett
took offense at Caleb ribbing him
'bout his face; not meaning no harm;
but Sprockett gunned him quicker
than Ma can gut and clean a catfish.

I enjoyed conversing with Caleb
whilst we rode, always stuff to agree on
and argue about, in a good-natured way.
But no more: and it's Sprockett's fault,
for being so prickly 'bout his looks.

Shoot, he should wear a sack over his head,
so as not to scare women, children,
and anyone with a frail heart.

Still, when we raid Federal settlements,
I can't wait to see the faces of those whores
and their bastard sprats when they get
a first good glance at him; I'll wager
they drop dead at the sight
of that nightmare on horseback,
and save us the expense
of buying lead for bullets.

Ezekiel Smith, on Seeing John Sprockett in the Camp of Captain William Quantrill

Til he muttered his name,
I thought him a monster
rose from the grave,
his face grizzly-ripped,
but healed up best
as he'll ever be: his face
forever a nightmare
I try not to wince at.

I remember him from back
in Turpin, the minister's stepson;
he beat Preacher to death
after that man of God
killed Sprockett's Ma
for a whore, though I heard
she never traipsed about after
they was yoked, though that made
no never mind to Preacher,
perched so high in Heaven,
only Jesus was above him.

At first, I thought to warn
the Captain not to trust Sprockett:
an outsider, and maybe that gouging
hid an Abolitionist spy.
But when I heard his name,
I knew him for one of us,
and when he testified the Injun
saved his life, good enough for me.

From what I hear about how
he sent to Hell that posse
seeking to avenge the Preacher,
I know he'll be badger-fierce
when we twister-hit Lawrence,
the Kansas capital and unholy
abolitionist Jerusalem.

Mrs. Lydia Watson, Southern Sympathizer

Whenever I hear of the exploits
of gallant Captain Quantrill's band,
I cheer and shake fists at Federal troops.

"Kill the usurpers," I penned in a letter
to my sister: her reply scandalized me:

"I fear this conflict will end in tragedy,
dear Sister: brother murdering brother,
father armed against son, friend butchering
lifelong friend. I grieve for our country!"

"Then either you haven't suffered,"
I fired back, "from Federal armies,
or, Sister, you bless their foul cause.
Here, we are besieged by invaders
threatening to unleash our slaves on us:
vengeful wolf packs of rapine and murder."

So I wrote back, then looked outside;
a company under the command of valiant
Quantrill paraded by, doffing floppy-brimmed
hats like Cavaliers, before they galloped off,
futilely pursued by a mob of Union regulars:
buzzards stripping the countryside.

When my Henry joined to battle the Visigoths,
I echoed the Spartan mother who told her son:

"Return with your shield or on it."
For an instant I detected Henry's sickly smile,
to be faced with that choice that true heroes,
like William Quantrill, never fret about.

Frank James Explains One Source of Quantrill's Success to New Recruit, John Sprockett

Like as not, you've seen we ride the finest mounts.
Let's just say the Captain has as good an eye
for prime horseflesh as a thieving Pawnee.

The quality of our steeds is a big part of why
we can raid with daring: not a Union mount
can run with us, once we put spurs to flanks.

Useless for Federal farmers to try to hide
their best horses; we've already sniffed out
where those swift steppers are cached; only fair

for us to free those steeds from farmers who claim
they own those horses that long to be ridden fast
and wild as prairie fires by Missouri patriots.

'Course, Confederate farmers donate their best
stock, and sometimes we buy promising mounts,
though right-minded folk are happy

to make gifts of their prime horseflesh, to ensure
our continued freedom from the tyranny of Federals,
who'd like to put us all in chains and free our darkies:

thus committing the sin of upsetting Jesus' order.

John Sprockett Observes the Drawn Battle Lines

Either you sign up to fight for the Union
or you're put under house arrest for treason.
So far soldiers ain't so eager to confront me:
One look at my face, they swallow
like a bug's stuck in their throats,
then they back out of my company, slow
as if a rattler's in their path, afraid
I'll shoot them for their discourtesy
of staring, which I just might.

Besides, it's common knowledge
I ride with Quantrill, so most folks
leave me be: raiding vents my rage
over what that bear did to me.
Still, some Abolitionist farms
we've burned were neighbors
who fed me slices of pie as a lad,
when I looked like an ordinary boy
who might find a girl who smiled
sweet as peach cobbler at me.

My one chance at that?
When Sarah and I sparked,
despite her Pa hating me for not being rich,
and more, for not being the Bible-legal
son of Pa, a preacher: who saw evil
in every inch of me. But Sarah's dead.

Much as I mourn and grieve
and silently cry myself to sleep,
I thank Jesus she can't see the monster
I've become, with this face; worse,
with being a bushwhacking killer.

When the black cloud twisters and roars
inside my head, I'm a slave to the rage
and murder that side-winds out of me,

though all I ever wanted
was to get along with folks
or just to be left alone.

John Sprockett Thinks about the Kansas City Jail Incident

Fellas mutter about McCorkle's sister
and the other women held prisoner
in the Kansas City jail: decoys
to flush out brothers and husbands
who raid Federal strongholds.

"The Abolitionists blew up the jail!"
Zeke spits into the crackling flames,
"murdering those big-hearted gals."
Others fire sidearms into the sky,
like stars are Federal bushwhackers.

I'm in a fantod too, even if new to this band.
Ever since Ma was killed by my preacher
step-daddy, I don't abide insults nor injuries
to women. Still, when I calm down a mite,
I wonder how these boys know
it wasn't just an awful accident.
They talk of killing every Blue Belly
in Kansas and Missouri: Hell,
in the whole damn country.
Looking like a monster, I don't need
much goading to shoot and shout,

"Damn Lawrence to Perdition!"

That's where we're riding, to burn
the Federals' capital and plug
every Abolitionist thinking he's safe
as a mountain from the likes of us.

Just please, Jesus, let us be right.

After His First Foray with Quantrill's Raiders, John Sprockett Considers His Situation

Some would say I'm lucky
that grizzly's claws missed my eyes.
More like, why couldn't that bear
have killed me and rid the world
of one more monster: murder's
the only way I can dowse the flames
of rage that fly out of me like buzzards
thudding and tearing atop a dead mule.
And now, under Captain Quantrill,
we're galloping for this Free Stater farm.

Bile scorches my throat: everything
in my head goes black as the smoke
of Perdition, while we circle the sod hut,
whoop like massacre-crazed Injuns, toss
lassos over the mounts, shoot the livestock,
smoke out the family and gun the farmer
and his sons. Jesus help his wife and daughter.
Afterwards, I stare at what we've done.

Though I can't look like I pity Unionists,
these folks didn't do nothing to me,
but will weigh on my soul
'til I'm summoned to battle Pa
in a boxing ring of brimstone, forever.

Gone-Nose, after the Raid on a Unionist Farm

Does the whites' Jesus smile
at their slaughtering this farm family?
All of these riders pray to their Jesus
every morning before mounting up,
and he preached love for all,
yet they kill as easily as passing wind,
which tells me that their Jesus
loves noting more than hypocrites.

My blood was singing, to join
their raid on an enemy; our tribe, too, keeps
slaves, the spoils of plunder and trade.

The white I saved from that bear
before we joined these raiders was fierce
to kill the men, but refused to mount the women.

When one raider buttoned his britches,
spat, and called the women, "Abolitionist whores,"
which even without knowing their strange tongue,
I could tell was a curse of great power,

Skull stopped the other from using
his knife on the mother and sobbing daughter:
breaking the man's wrist, and kicking him
to the ground, daring the others
to go against him, his ruined face
too powerful a medicine to battle.

I do not understand him: the women
of enemies are to be used as we please,
but he holds them superior to warriors,
though we are the ones who bring in game
and steal horses, a tribe's true wealth.

Gone-Nose, after the Raid on the Unionist Farm, II

My head-splitter was about
to smash the farmer,
when the white demons
shot him and his family;
we rode off before
I could take scalps.

The raiders hated them
for holding no slaves,
as I hated the riders:
not trusting me with a handgun
or musket, though except
for Skull's repeater,
I can send arrows
thudding into a body
faster than any single-shot.

After the farm was ashes,
Skull cursed like Wendigo,
kicked the male corpses,
the others backing away,
fearing he'd kill them all.

In their camp, the others
drank burning-lance-water
and boasted of their courage
in killing women, a girl-child,
and small boys.

Skull sat apart, and though
he drank, made no loud,
happy boasts, only muttered,

struck his chest, his head,
as if begging the gods'
forgiveness, for the blood
he'd shed: tormented
by the spirits of those he's killed:
stealing lives that never
did him any harm.

III—The Hell Road to Lawrence

On the Way to Lawrence, John Sprockett Ponders Slavery

No one we knew owned slaves,
'cept one shopkeeper in Turpin;
Mr. Ludlow worked that poor woman
half to death, beat her for no reason
'cept meanness, had his way with her,
his wife visiting her sister over to Illinois.

To keep the peace with his missus,
he sold Esther downriver; she killed
herself rather than feel the overseer's
bullwhip in the back-breaking cotton fields.
Grieved me to tears, her a soft spoken,
sad-smiling woman, quoting poetry
by the mile, even better than me.
Lord knows where she picked up the gift.

Him and his wife left town soon after;
lucky for them, for I'd begun to hatch a plan;
still, what happened to Esther made me see
how wrong it was to own another man;
worse, a woman, and force her to do things
only folks in love have a right to.

So why, I keep asking myself,
am I riding with Border Ruffians,
to wipe out Lawrence, a prairie paradise
of brotherhood? Only answer I got:
us Missouri boys can't let outsiders
tell us what to do, though I know
I'll be doomed to Hell, for stomping out
all those innocent lives.

Riding to Lawrence, John Sprockett Remembers His Beloved Sarah

So much has happened, nary any of it good—
since that night Sarah died in her birth blood
in that leaking, ghost-breath barn—that I've not
had a chance to think of her, let alone mourn,
'til now, riding to Lawrence to do bloody work.

Sarah had a laugh silvery as a music box,
a smile sweeter than penny candy,
the face of an angel, but the heart of an imp
when she'd side-wind a leg around mine,
and hold onto my waist, to spin my head.
Her eyes misted when I recited poetry
and the verses I wrote just for her,
lines I murmur now, to bring back her face.

I fall back to the rear, and sob into my chest
so the others can't see me, to remember
her going into labor in that barn we sheltered in,
from her flint-hearted Pa, and my heartless one.
I couldn't stop the blood, but held our precious
mite of a baby girl and held Sarah too;
her breaths rasped like a prison file, then silent.

Then the Sheriff cold-cocked me. Had I not
escaped, he'd have seen me jerked to Jesus.
I'd've been honored to spend my life
taking care of Sarah and our daughter.
But I've become a man as expert at killing
as a fiddler can scrape out tunes folks dance to
like they've been summoned by Old Jack Scratch
Himself. Just a matter of time before that Trickster
and Liar summons me to toil in his evil dancehall
when my murderous life's over.

John Sprockett Remembers His Stepfather, the Reverend Jeremiah Sprockett

Pa loved his Bible more than family,
fond of quoting Jesus as admonishing,
"Slaves, obey your masters," whenever
he'd lend me out to neighbor farmers
and take my wages as his preacher-due.
He backhanded me the one time
I pointed out it wasn't Jesus, but Paul,
who'd said that, and if Jesus had a thought
on the subject it was probably that all
of us had a right to breathe the free air.

Despite that mistake, Pa was forever
quoting Scripture for proof I was damned,
being spawn of Ma taking comfort
with a peddler before Pa was on the scene.

When I wasn't laboring for others,
I plowed, scythed, and fed our stock;
I liked the work a sight more than fidgeting
through his Sunday sermons that were longer
than the New Testament, when the Old One
had all the good smitings and grand poetry,
like Ruth pledging to Naomi:

"Where thou goest, I will go…"

which always tears me up like I'd sliced
an onion big as a melon: at Ruth's devotion
to a woman she loved like her own mother,
and for Ruth being a stranger in Canaan.

I'm a stranger everywhere: for killing Pa
after what he did to Ma, and for taking care
of the posse that wanted to jerk me to Jesus
for Pa's worthless, hypocrite, murderous sake.

What with the scars that grizzly ripped
down my face, you could say I'm Cain,
'cept those marks don't protect me,
just make everyone want to send me to Hell,
where I know I belong, but not just yet.

William Quantrill, on the Road to Lawrence, Kansas, Inspects the Perdee Farm

James's farmhouse sits on high ground,
giving us a view of any dastardly
Federals trying to sneak up on us.
Plus the east bank of the Blackwater—
where the Blue Bellies would cross—
is too steep for an easy dash.

From here, we'll ride west for Lawrence,
where godless whites and blacks grunt
together without slaves, anathema to Jesus.

They'll pay for what happened
in the Kansas City jail: our women locked up
on false charges: Yankee bastards
set fire to the building, laughed to watch
those valiant ladies burn: may their shrieks
hound their killers 'til Satan drags 'em to Hell.

James Perdee's a true believer: his sons
joining our righteous band to help keep
Missouri a proud slave state, making sure
Abraham "Traitor" Lincoln—that tall drink
of dirty Washington water—fails in this war.

We'll rest the horses and men at Perdee's,
get provisioned from James's generous stores
and those of other farmers loyal to our cause.
We'll force landowners who support the Unionists
to contribute 'til they bleed, then ride at dawn,
and when we get to Ben Potter's farm,

I'll announce my plans for Lawrence,
that Sodom of godless comingling.
The Lord may have pity on those sinners;
but we'll not show them the least mercy.

Martin Rice, after Refusing to Help Provision William Quantrill's Raider's

Those Secesh rode into my front yard
like they owned it, Quantrill shouting
I had to provision his renegades
so those heartless marauders
could raze Abolitionist Lawrence.

"To protect us white folks from slavery
at the hands of rebel slaves."

I spat a chaw at his dusty boots.

"I'll not abet slave holders nor traitors.
What have the folks of Lawrence done
to varmints like you?" I commenced
whittling again, but Quantrill dragged me
into my own yard and flung me down.

"Get your women cooking, or by God,
your Federal carcass will decorate the nearest tree."
My Minnie skittered past him, helped me rise.

"Do as he says," she pleaded. I chafed
for my sidearm, but Quantrill kicked me
in the butt, so I spun to give him the licking
of his worthless life, but his .44 poked my nose.

When I get the chance, I'll turn him into
a leaky crimson pail, or watch him swing,
crows and buzzards closing in for the feast.

They were riders from Hell, one in particular:
half his face bear ripped, too terrifying
to argue with, so I nodded to Minnie,
though I hated myself for giving in.

Benjamin Potter Hears of William Quantrill's Treatment of Martin Rice

I gladly provision the Captain
for his raid on Lawrence:
Federals I don't know or care about,
But I'll not abide his ill-treatment
of my neighbor and friend Martin Rice,
and told William so, even if he stared
a lead-filled blizzard at me
for siding with a Blue Belly.

Without Martin, my wheat
would've been twister-trampled.
He treats my horses for colic,
and most of all, his Minnie saw
my youngest into this world
when the midwife couldn't
reach us in time: Martin and me
crying and laughing afterwards,
out of joy and relief.

So when Quantrill beat Martin
into agreeing to provision his raid,
I told William I was done with him
if it happened again; me with the men
and guns to back up the threat.

Raiders get bushwhacked all the time,
but you can depend on neighbors,
even if you disagree on everything
'cept the weather: how folks survive
out here on the wind-and-hail plains
even if you ain't fast friends,
like Martin and me are.

Benjamin Potter, Southern Sympathizer, Faces Execution

No trial, no judge, nor jury
nor folks putting in a good word—
'cept Martin Rice, our Unionist neighbor,
telling the General I'm not one
to take up arms against the Union,
though he was laughed at, and when
he wouldn't stop begging for my life,
was told he was parlous close
to being a traitor and to shut up, or else
he could join me and the others
on the creaking, makeshift scaffold—
I'm frog marched to this field
with five neighbors of a like mind,
for "Giving aid to enemy marauders."

Enemy? Good men fighting the one way
they know how, for what they believe in.
When Jayhawkers and Union troops
torch our houses and crops, steal our livestock
and anything that ain't nailed down,
it's to restore the Union?

Trudy's sobbing, my boys stony as walls;
they'll ride with Quantrill, to avenge me,
Trudy most likely thrown off the farm,
though Martin swears he'll take care of her,
a good man, even if a Federal. Or maybe
she can move back to Louisville, to her sister.
What galls most? We don't even own slaves,
but don't abide being told what to do.

"Last words?" the officer barks.

"Long live the Confederacy!" I shout,
the boys hurrah and try to raise fists,
but our wrists are tied behind our backs,
lest we rush the execution squad,
neighbors killing neighbors:
the worst kind of war there is.

Martin Rice, at the Execution of Benjamin Potter

Least I could do,
after Ben saved me
from a second beating
by Quantrill, was to stand
in that field and salute
my dear friend, my protests
to the General availing Ben
not even a delay.

But now, he's been marched
to a field with other Confederates,
and hanged. I'm Union,
but our Army's making no friends
with their own terror tactics.

And I've lost a damn fine friend.
When his girls and our wives
cleared the table after Sunday dinners,
he and I'd sneak off to the barn
for his scorching home brew
that made me vision daytime comets.

After I paid my sad respects
to his widow and grown sons,
who all glowered at me
as if I'd tightened the noose,

I rode home slow, mourning
a new emptiness in my life,
and fearing that Quantrill'd
blame me for Ben's execution,

and exact punishment
like a bullwhip-wielding
Egyptian overlord.

John Sprockett Looks Behind, As Quantrill's Raiders Ride for Lawrence

Kansas Cavalry's dust plume pursues us,
though they'll never catch up before we punish
Lawrence for its Abolitionist ways. Still,
part of me wants those horsemen to ride down
our tails: guilt for what we're about to do,
but also wanting an old-fashioned fight,
not wolves blood-drunk on sheep
bleating while their throats are ripped.

I want men to fight back, want to smell
black powder heavy as a spring storm,
to feel my blade rip a man's gut, before
he can do the same to me, not an old timer,
his hands too crippled to fire a musket,
or women and girls begging for the mercy
of not being done over by men whose blood's
wild as a splay-taloned eagle on a mouse.

I want to make men suffer, for that grizzly
raking my face like a plow breaking up clumps
of winter soil ahead of the spring planting,
want to feel the wind of musket balls crease
the air like April's sweetest breezes,
want to ride into battle like a Comanche warrior
and count coup against a worthy enemy,
not be a marauder slaughtering innocents,
to bring Jesus' wrath down on me for all time.

Let me not look back again, for fear
of being turned into a Pillar of Salt,
just ride forward, toward the task at hand.

Gone-Nose Contemplates the Raid on Lawrence

After they're all dead, these enemies
of the whites I ride with, I'll take guns,
blankets, bright necklaces and bracelets:
to give my kinsman, so I may be let back
into my tribe, and not have to ride
with these whites, whose throats

I'd have gladly slashed after
they'd offered me liquor and laughed
to see me stumble like a wind-crazed leaf
in the Moon of the Golden Trees,
laughed, too, to trip me when I collect wood
for cook fires, or when they refuse to share
the meat they took from a farmer,
as if Comanches, who believe, as do whites,
all of Turtle's creation belongs to them.

With the warriors of my band,
I'd bring terror to these whites' drunken sleep.
When they raid this place they call "Lawrence,"
and while smoke and screams choke the air,
I might kill as many marauders as I can,
before riding fast for my tribe's summer camp.

If Skull wishes to ride with me, he's welcome.
If not, I'll ride alone; and if he tries to stop me,
more loyal to these whites than to me,
who saved him, nursed him back to health,
I'll slash the throat of that killer
possessed by the spirit of the bear
that now lives in rage inside him.

Millie Spangler, Ten-Years-Old, Spots John Sprockett among Quantrill's Raiders

When they stopped to water their horses,
I saw it was true about him: Satan's scarred face;
folks claim it was from a grizzly he killed
with his bare hands. Still, one more instant
of gawking, and I'd've gagged up the honey-
slathered slab of bread, oven-warm, Ma gave me,
while I cheered our Secesh boys going into battle
against those thieving Lawrence Abolitionists.

None of the others' gallantry about him,
just a sadness in even the good side of his face,
though our cause is just and the Unionists
have to be punished: least, what Pa says,
though my best friend's Hattie Morris,
and her and her folks claim it ain't right
for some to own others, which to hear them
sorta makes sense, 'til I get home to Ma and Pa.

I wish Mr. Sprockett was stage-actor handsome,
so I could dream, all warm, about him
and his sorrows, 'stead of being scared worse
than of falling into the pigsty. When he spied me
staring, he smiled and flourished his hat, valiant
as Captain Quantrill: made him look even scarier.

John Sprockett Listens to William Quantrill's Speech Before the Raid on Lawrence

"Spare no one!" Captain shouts,
us cheering, though Abolitionists
didn't murder my poetry-loving Ma.
Nor did they shoot my sweet kid brother Ned
nor murder Miz Wilton, who took us in
when that posse wanted me exalted
Nor did the folks of Lawrence magic
that bear to scrape my face
like a rake through mud.

Still, bile rises like a cougar's scream:
Captain swears it's our sacred duty
to take vengeance for Jay Hawkers
burning farmhouses, leaving women,
children, and farmers bullet-ripped,
and worse. Captain's but the spark
to the straw of our rage, though
I'll carry the guilt of this killing
the rest of my days. May they be short.

Women shriek at my face when I offer
to carry their parcels; parents threaten
I'll eat their children, if they don't behave.

Maybe some Lawrence Abolitionist
will get off a lucky shot, and send me
to Hell: which will be nothing
but endless rooms full of mirrors
I can never shut my eyes to.

John Sprockett and Quantrill's Raiders Ride Deeper into Kansas

Union troops make no effort to engage us
when we ride past, outnumbering them
three-to-one, though if I led that cavalry,
I'd have kicked my mount's withers
into a gallop and done all I could to stop
what everyone knows will be a slaughter.

They just sit their mounts at the top of a rise;
some of our boys flourish their hats,
gallant as if parading past ladies fluttering
lace handkerchiefs to wish us victory.
After a few more hours of steady riding,
I turn again, see a dust plume, but no way
can they catch us now, and no taste for a fight.

While we ride, I keep hoping the boys won't do
to defenseless women and girls what I can't abide.
Even looking like a nightmare on horseback,
I've a soft spot for the ladies, though none
can behold my face without shrieking.

Thinking of the likely outcome of our raid,
my blood boils, both because I've an appetite
for savagery now that the only men who'll ride
with or abide me are marauders and bushwhackers.
Plus, my rage rises like a snarling wolf against
these boys I accompany, should they dare the dirty.

Killing armed men's one thing. Doing women over
for the evil fun of it, neither Jesus nor I will forgive.

Stephen J. Wilson, Sixteen, Clerk at B.J. Pettibone's Dry Goods, Gardner, Kansas

We were closing for the evening,
Mr. Pettibone praising my ciphering
faster than the Pony Express
and helpful to the female customers,

when that damn Secesh devil,
Quantrill and his bully-boys rode up,
and like Greeks stripping Troy
that we learned about in Miz McCreary's
classroom, cleared out all the canned goods
from the shelves, for their murdering
Confederate bellies, seized bolts of cloth
for their whores, and all our guns, muskets,
and ammunition, to use for butchery.

They forced Mr. Pettibone to gee up
one provision-heavy wagon, to dissuade pursuit.
Lord, don't let them shoot him!
Word's spread they gun down guides
who don't know the route, and some who do,
and leave them for the buzzards, coyotes
and crows, 'til kin find their skeletons.

Then there was that one hell rider,
looked like he shaved with barbed wire,
didn't join in the general despoliation,
just sat his mount like Satan's archangel,
making sure everything got stolen.
Without saying a word, he scared me more
than the others that were shouting threats.

I've no stomach for Ma's stew tonight,
'sides, she shakes too hard to ladle it out.

John Sprockett Keeps Watch As Quantrill's Raiders Strip B.J. Pettibone's Store

Not as a look-out for townsfolk
or militias frothing for vengeance,
or Cavalry counter-attacking,
though that's what the Captain
ordered me to do: but to see
that none of our band takes liberties
with the Missus or daughters,
like what happened when we raided
that farm for provisions.

The one good thing
about my bear-ruined face:
it makes most men's knees shimmy
like quaking aspen in a blizzard:
afraid I'll blast 'em
for their bad manners of gawking.

I may be a monster to look at,
and sometimes do kill men
for no reason 'cept meanness
for being turned into an ogre,
but I'll never let any harm
come to the ladies,
like if these boys try the dirty
with Mrs. Pettibone and her girls.

The Captain took him hostage,
told me when we're far enough
from town, to shove him into the brush
and make a widow of his Missus,
orphans of his daughters.

His blood another anvil on my soul.

B.J. Pettibone Taken Hostage

They'll blow out my lamp
now they know I've less idea
of how to get these murderers
to Lawrence, than the route
to New York City. My killer?
That hell-fiend John Sprockett:
so brimstone-fierce, even
these Secesh scum wince at the rage
that roars out of him and slam shut
their eyes at his grizzly-ripped face.

I fight tears, at never seeing my wife
and daughters again, Quantrill nodding
to Sprockett to yank me off the wagon,
heavy with goods they stole from my store,
and force me to walk into the shoulder-
high buffalo grass, until he tells me to stop,
and I start to cry, much as I'd wished
to meet Judgment brave as St. Peter.

"Shut up," he stuffs a dirty bandana
into my mouth, knocks me down
and fires into the buffalo-grass soil.
"That was for the sake of your wife
and daughters. Stay still 'til you can't
see or hear us no more," and rides back
to those thieving killers.

So after I stop pissing myself,
I'm thinking you can't judge a man
folks claim's a monster, when maybe
he's tired of his murdering ways.

That, and how I can't wait to fill
my arms with Claire, Isabella,
and Melissa, and never let them go.

John Sprockett and the No Longer Useful Guides

That first time I was ordered to shoot
an Abolitionist we'd kidnapped,
and leave him in the buffalo grass,
I couldn't, even with my reputation
for rage: him with a wife and two daughters.
Besides he sat stoic as the Baptist
about to lose his holy head
when we shoved him onto the lead wagon
loaded with provisions we'd taken
from his dry goods store and told him
to guide us: knowing what would happen
when he grew unsure of the route.

But like I said, he went quiet as a spy
caught behind enemy lines, so's I couldn't
back-shoot him, let alone full in his face,
that, unlike mine, wasn't a nightmare.
When I marched him into the long grass,
I knocked him down, blasted into
the ground, and told him if he wanted
no holes in his head or elsewhere,
to lie still for a good ten minutes.

But the next time, Captain sent
Ben Sanders with me. Afterward,
he kicked the corpse like a tin can
and unbuttoned his trousers to piss on
"The no-good, slave-loving sumbitch."

"Don't," I said soft as windless snow.
Sanders backed away, told the Captain
the job was done, 'cept the shot'll
echo in my head 'til the day I die.

The third time, I didn't hesitate.

Isaiah Templeton, Forced To Guide Quantrill's Raiders

I knew what happens to Union men
grabbed to guide these guerilla scum
to raid Lawrence, so I figured
if I'm already dead but still walking,
I'd send these murderers
on a wild goose chase.

"Just a little farther," I pointed,
hoping that maybe the Kiowa raiders
that sometimes marauded farms
would want the wagons
these Secesh rats had stolen,
and maybe, just maybe,
I could sneak off amidst
the gunfire and flaming arrows,
or steal a mount,
and if not, grab a sidearm
and take some bastards with me.

But they lost patience,
and Quantrill nodded
to that bear-ripped hell fiend,
John Sprockett. He gun-nudged me
into the silent buffalo grass:
lucky I'd no wife or kids
to mourn me, nor for me
to cry over at never seeing again.

"Bad luck," he mumbled,
"I got used to killing unarmed men.
At least, you'll end up in Heaven,
whilst me . . ." he shrugged.

His bullet knocked me down,
stole my breath, wearied me
more than if I'd not slept
in a hundred years.

Outside Lawrence, Kansas: Gone-Nose Leaves Quantrill's Raiders

I'll not wait until after the raid to leave with booty,
for these whites think it funny as Coyote
to give me lightning water. I pretend to drink,
pretend to reel like a bison with the falling sickness.

When they try to get me to drink more,
I climb a tree, so after they drink themselves
into a stinking sleep, I creep to their mounts,
take the two fastest, a musket, a shot pouch,

a blade bigger than Wendigo's root,
enough revolvers for my band,
some trade blankets and necklaces
sacred to their god, Jesus Christ.

I whisper soothing words and place
hands over the mounts' muzzles,
lead them off quiet as grass in still weather.
Before I ride away, the white I call "Skull"—

the one I saved from that great bear—
raises a hand in thanks and farewell:
unlikely we'll meet this side of the Land
of Good Hunting. Then I'm gone, no one

sounding the alarm, nor cutting me off,
these whites too drunk to wake.
Clear of their camp, I mount and walk
until we're a safe distance away,

then kick my horse's withers,
to make for my tribe's summer grounds,
and hope the goods I've taken will pay
my debt for lying with my kinsman's woman,

though living alone might be simpler, safer.

John Sprockett Watches Gone-Nose Leave Quantrill's Camp

Moving silent as a twirling leaf,
Gone-Nose mounts the Captain's favorite.
I could pick him off from my bed roll,
but I owe him my life, though I'd almost
as soon be dead than look like this,
a little girl's nightmare-monster.

Him and me got swept into Quantrill fever
when the Captain and his raiders rode
into our camp while I was healing up.
They made it plain as horse manure
if we didn't join, we'd be killed slow.

Besides, I'd known most of his men
from when we were all boys in Missouri,
not so many years back, though it seems
longer than a life sentence of breaking rocks
in the state penitentiary: so many deaths
hanging, howling, from my soul.

And now at dawn, we raid Lawrence,
I might've joined Gone-Nose and escaped
the rivers of bloodletting, but I'll stand
by these boys, though I can't say
I'd want any of them as pards for life.

And partaking of the slaughter will forfeit me
any chance of meeting up with Ma, Ned,
Miz Wilton and my darling sweetheart Sarah,
once Jesus judges what I've done.

Before the Raid on Lawrence, Quantrill Wakes to Find His Favorite Mount Gone

Damn that thieving red savage,
stealing my best horse that I took off
a Federal farmer: that mare never
came up lame, no matter how hard
I rode her, and a gait smooth
as fresh churned butter.
If I get my hands on that Skin,
I'll kill him slow, like Comanches do
to foes that ain't showed enough grit.

I bet Sprockett knows where he went,
them being pards when we forced them
to join our righteous Secesh cause.
But Sprockett's the one man I'm a-feared of,
with his grizzly-slashed face and temper
that could murder the whole damned state
if pushed the least bit over the line
of what he considers common courtesy,
like gawking at him or insulting ladies—
even Abolitionist harlots—or not listening,
when he recites poetry by the bushel.
Glad as I am to have that crazed killer
with us, I'd be happy if he rode off.

Now I'm burning over my stolen mount,
plus another nag that Injun took, and guns,
ammunition, and provisions we forced
Federal farmers to hand over. I'll kill
that Skin and whoever was supposed
to be on guard duty when he rode off.

Raiders? Shoot, more like dreamland babies
after sucking on their mommas' titties
and being washed in warm baths.

But Lawrence'll pay, I'll make sure of that.

John Sprockett Hears William Quantrill's Speech before the Raid on Lawrence

"Kill all the men and boys!"
he roars like a hellfire
Old Testament prophet.

"Vengeance for our wives
and sisters murdered
in the Kansas City jail,
the fire and explosion
planned and carried out
by Jay Hawkers, to poke
a big, burning stick
into the eyes of us Secesh!"

In a fury, we mount,
to leave no male alive,
not a building standing,
just smoldering slats
toppling in a breeze.

Only savagery calms
the wolves snarling
inside me,
and only for a little while.

I check my sidearm,
my Spenser repeating rifle,
and kick my mount
into a frothing gallop,
and like the others bit
by murder-fever, ride
like the wrath of God.

Or more likely,
the rage of Satan.

IV—The Raid

Mrs. Millie Holcomb Witnesses the Shooting of Her Husband and Son

It was an ordinary summer morning,
warm breezes swaying the wheat
while I shelled peas and hummed a hymn.
Hiram scything, Isaac bundling the sheaves,
when I spied swirling dust. I should've
known it wasn't a waterspout over our pond
or a dust devil, but Satan-Quantrill,
and his demons, my husband and son falling,
Secesh killers riding past, raising mocking hats,
as if the Union cavalry saluting a lady
who applauded their gallantry.

I ran screaming to where my husband
and darling boy lay, blood puddling
like bison-trampled prairie mud.
Abraham, our black hired hand, working
in the barn, flew fast as a falcon, listened
to their chests, tried to stop the spate,
and to keep me from the awful sight.

I batted away his hands, pleaded for them
to breathe, to laugh at their bad joke,
while I howled and howled, and, I confess
to my shame, blamed, hated Abraham.

He let me cry, hit him with my small fists,
then through his own tears, he laid my men
gentle as babies on the kitchen table,
to clean them for a decent burial;
soon we heard more shots, us two shuddering,
sobbing, knowing there'd be a need
for graves upon graves upon graves.

Abraham Jones, Hired Hand on the Holcomb Farm

I thought I'd seen all there was of cruelty
when I was a house slave, serving *them* meals
that could've fed the Quarters all week.
They sold the woman I loved and thought
I'd married, along with our daughter:
him explaining, shame-faced-drunk,
he was in difficulties, as an excuse.

I could've burned down their mansion,
or poisoned or stabbed or strangled them,
when word drifted back on a bad wind,
that Ophelia and Callie were dead.

'Stead, I studied the maps in the library
he drank in, and didn't head north
into noose-tossing slave catchers,
but made my way west to Free Kansas
found honorable work with the Holcombs.

But now Hiram and his son Isaac
have been killed by Quantrill's Secesh-devils.
When I finished digging the graves
and spoke a few words over that good man
and fine boy, Mrs. Holcomb's knees gave way.
I tried to hold her up, but she leapt back
from a rattler, then begged me to forgive her.

"Nothing to forgive," I murmured,
"you've suffered enough already,"

but I could see she blamed me, a black man,
for Hiram and Isaac's murders.
Better if she goes to her sister in Chicago
I'll try to find a town rumored
to be run by them like me.

The Raid on Lawrence, Kansas: William Quantrill

We rode out of the East, sun blinding
those slave-loving devils daring
to consort with and arm blacks,
like they were real Americans,
with a right to defend themselves.

My orders: kill every man and boy,
black or white. After we'd shot them
in the streets, we stormed their homes
and shops, gunned them in front
of their shrieking women: up to me,
we'd have shot those Unionist harlots too.

But that bear-ripped devil, Sprockett,
swore he'd not let any man live
who took a female's life.

"Men are fair game, but ladies are sacred;
if any are touched, you'll answer to me,"
he swore, crazed as the bear that'd furrowed
his face like a plow pulled by a drunk mule.

Still, it gave me pleasure to gun
their minister; he'd preached the mingling
of the races was what Jesus intended.

Not a male escaped, 'cept that butcher,
General Jim Lane; who yellow bellied
through a cornfield in his nightshirt,
before we could leave him for the crows.
He'll spread word of what to expect
if anyone dares go against us.

We left the town a Halloween bonfire,
cleansed the stain of their sinful commingling,
when Jesus had commanded,

"Slaves, obey your masters!"
If anyone dares declare He didn't say it,
I'll plug the lying, blasphemous bastard.

Sally McWhorter, School Teacher, Faces Down One of Quantrill's Raiders

I never counted myself lucky before,
my face plain as a tin plate: teaching
my one choice, mother to a schoolroom,
but no sons of my own, thank Jesus,
to be shot by Secesh butchers.
But a barbarian rides into my school,
the coward ordering me to stand aside,
so he can murder all the boys.

I stand up to my too-tall-to-be-courted
height, and spit at this rider,
with his face so bear-raked, it takes
all my courage to stare him down,

"If you want to murder these blameless
angels, you will have to kill me first."
That stopped the devil dead in his tracks.
Still, I suppose even the most heartless
of demons has a dim memory of the mother
who raised him, of a beloved younger sister.
For the monster bowed gallant as a Cavalier,

"Ma'am, I apologize, there will be
no further mayhem in here today,"
and recited Portia, on the quality of mercy,
my mouth wider than a famished nestling,
to hear the Bard from the lips of a murderer
who looked like he'd ridden into Kansas
straight from the stables of Hell.

He whirled his mount and was gone;
I gathered the children and hugged them,
to make sure we were all still alive: silent tears
etching my cheeks, not caring that Mother,
a beauty in her time, scolded that crying,

"Never did a homely thing like you any good."

Christopher McPherson, Twelve-Year-Old Schoolboy

I always thought church and school
wastes of time: fishing's a lot more fun
than being hollered at 'bout sin and Hell
and Jesus' love, or Miz McWhorter's letters
and cyphering, when I'd no plans to read
a single book, not even the Good One,
once I escaped her schoolhouse forever.

But when she stood up to that Secesh
grizzly-gouged monster, his gun cocked
to kill us boys, and us too scared to rush him
and grab his side arm and repeater,
or even to run like rabbits for their warrens,
and when she scolded he'd have to kill her
to get to us, he liked to cry a hailstorm
at the thought of shooting a woman,
then quoted from that Bard feller Miz McWhorter's
always going on about, like he's as smart
as President Lincoln and Frederick Douglass.

Anyway, Miz McWhorter saved our lives;
to repay her I'll listen in class from now on,
not crack jokes about useless books,
when they're why I'm still standing,
though I'm trembling and tripping
over feet suddenly too big for me.

Big Bob Tolliver

Every Abolitionist bastard I shot,
I shouted, "This is for my sister,
as sweet a gal as ever drew breath,"
though I knew these particular
Abolitionists hadn't blown up
the Kansas City jail where she died.

Still, they were Federals, so high
and mighty about who we could own.
Where does it say we're all equal?
Not in the Constitution! And don't
Jesus declare, "Slaves, obey your masters."
But Jay Hawkers want to deprive us
of lawful property without paying us.

My one regret, that traitor Lincoln
wasn't there to be gunned down,
that ugly son-of-a-bitch waging war
on the South to "preserve the Union."

What he really wants? To enslave
good, Jesus-fearing white folks
and let slaves lay bullwhips to our backs:
against the natural order, since we
brought them from Africa to toil for us.

Besides, I don't own no slaves.
Well, maybe just one or two.

John Sprockett Goes His Own Way

First, we hit a farm just east of Lawrence:
a father and son—the boy no more than ten,
guilt sizzling my heart, but in war, I told myself,
even young-un's can aim a pistol or musket.
Their blood fountained, my heart throbbed
like the scars that grizzly slashed down my face.

The town lay open, men going about their business
with no thought this was their last morning on earth.
Two more fell to my gun, another; I stopped to reload,
and in that motionless moment, I saw the dead:
men, boys, two women. My fingers trembling,
I holstered my .44 at the third try, others shooting,
searching shops and homes for stragglers to kill.

The Captain dragged a minister into the street
and shot him like a dog, then signaled for me
to hunt down General Lane, running through
a wheat field, nightshirt flapping, sheaves higher
than his head, though I could follow
the shoved-aside stalks like the Sea
that parted for the Israelites,

'cept I let the General escape: Those five lives
I'd taken scorched my soul, like the witches'
cauldron in that play Ma loved, *Macbeth*.

"You let that murderer of good Missouri women
get away," the Captain thundered.

"I'm finished with killing," I stared
'til he looked away, like everyone does
when they see my grizzly-ripped face,

and know me to be just crazed enough
to plug him if he gave me the least cause.

He didn't, so I nudged my mount, hoping
if I rode high enough into the Rockies,
there'd be no one I'd have to slaughter,
when the storms inside my ruined head
spun and snaked like twisters.

Hattie Morris, Ten-Years-Old, as Quantrill's Raiders Return from the Raid on Lawrence

I stare down at them from our hill farm,
preening like Jesus had praised them
for shooting innocent men, women,
even kids like me, like frothing dogs:
just for believing there's no such thing
as masters or slaves.

I'm so mad I can't talk to Millie Spangler,
my best friend, leastways, before Killer Quantrill
brought hell to Lawrence and she gloated
they had it coming, for,

"Going against Jesus, Who said,
'Slaves obey your masters.'"

"Wasn't Jesus, but Paul," I sputtered,
and spat what we learned in Sunday School:
"'There is neither slave nor free man,
for we are all one in Jesus,'" or close enough.

"That ain't nothing but blasphemy,"
she shouted, "comparing them to us.
'Sides, they got it too good," Millie sniffed,
"three meals a day, and a place to sleep."

"You do stoop labor," I sneered, "and get
a bullwhip laid to your back if you stop
for the bittiest instant, and you watch
your husband get sent downriver
or your children sold, then you can snigger

how easy they got it," and I stalked off,
swearing I'd never speak to her again.
'Cept this far from town it's only her
and my dolly for company, though Dolly's
got the sense not to be so dumb.

V—Traveling Companions

Leaving Quantrill's Raiders, John Sprockett Comes Upon a Traveling Companion

She was squat as a cottonwood stump,
a skillet papoosed down her back.
I slowed, to offer her a ride,
Lawrence smoking behind us,
me with a heart heavy as a landslide,
at all the innocent blood I'd spilled there.

"I know you," she pointed, though hard
not to recognize my bear-ripped scars.
"One of Quantrill's murderers," she spat
forceful as a preacher ordering Satan off.

Those five souls—one a child, whose lives
I'd snuffed out—heavy as anvils.
I shrugged, nudged my mount into a trot,
no need to hear her cussing me any further.

"Hey," she yelled, "I'm tired of walking!"

"You're running from slavery, ain't you?"

"Mind your own damn business.
I seen what you done at that farm."

"If I could take that back . . ." I started.

"But you can't," she rasped.
"Now, help me up." I clasped
her work-hard hand, yanked her
behind me, and kicked my mount's
withers into a buttermilk canter,

heading West, away from Lawrence,
from Captain Quantrill and his men,
from the need to kill anyone else
in this damn dirty war.

John Sprockett and Sylvia Williams Ride West

Most wince at my face,
or train their eyes elsewhere,
so they don't have to see the gullies
that devil-bear clawed,
though Miz Williams ain't bothered,
but when I called her "Aunt Sylvie,"
she reached forward to grab my chin,
twisted me in the saddle, and spat,

"Call me by my slave name again,
and I'll cut your damn tongue out,
you Secesh murderer."

I apologized, and she allowed
as she'd been cook
on an Arkansas plantation,
the Master and his son killed
in the War, the Missus cruel
as a fairytale witch, trying to whip
Miz Williams once, but she grabbed
that rawhide rattler and smacked her
with the butt, so despite
my Confederate sympathies, I laughed.

"Others snuck off after dark,
I strode away in daylight,"
she confided, "took my skillet,
and what I figured I was owed
in wages that fanged female haint
kept from me all those years.
I'll open a restaurant and hotel,"
she nodded like it had already happened.

Her tale done, she demanded,
"What turned you into a Secesh devil?"

To pass the miles, I started with sad,
sweet Ma: "Abandoned by a drummer,
she had to get yoked to a preacher,
who needed a family so he could appear
respectable, but he couldn't keep
his fists off me, worse, off Ma;
he should've known I'd get too big
and mean, but he believed he'd invented
God's righteous wrath, so he kept at it,
to his sorrow," I sighed and summoned
up Ma's face from my memories.

"That don't explain nothin'. Keep going,"
Miz Williams prodded my spine.
I sighed and continued my sorry tale.

John Sprockett Continues Telling His Life Story to Sylvia Williams

"How'd you get to be such a heller,"
Miz Williams prodded, while we rode
leisurely as a Sunday buggy ride.
I started with how Sarah and me
tried to run away together, got
as far as a falling-down barn,
her dying in labor there,
though our baby lived.

I held the mite, and through my tears,
cooed her into a smiling sleep,
but Sarah's daddy had snuck up,
cold-cocked me, his posse
dragging me back to town,
for hanging. Instead, I grabbed
the new repeater the banker's son
had bragged on, knocked down a deputy
and rode like all of Hell
was howling for my soul.

"Still, I couldn't leave without
a quick goodbye to Ma,
but when I pulled up to the farm,
my preacher step-pa
was beating on her again,
him in a fantod over the posse
that couldn't keep me captured.

I made sure that was the last time
he ever hit her; my half-brother Ned
helped me bury her and toss him
to the hogs. Then we rode west,

took shelter with a young widow
who sensed we were desperadoes
but too kindly to care;
it burns my heart to ashes
she paid for her hospitality
when the posse murdered
her and Neddy, the best
brother in the world.

"I got vengeance on those varmints,
'cept the Sheriff, a decent man
forced into a dirty job by Sarah's Pa.
After the smoke cleared, I buried Ned
and Miz Wilton, left the rest
for the buzzards, sent the Sheriff
back to Missouri, him agreeing
it was safer to let me be."

"You're a heller, all right,"
Miz Williams observed,
"but you've had cause."
When I reined in for the night.
I shared out cold bacon
and cornbread, afraid a fire
might draw the Captain
and his raiders, them deserving
to have Federals gun them down.

Well, so do I.

Sylvia Williams Rides behind John Sprockett

I seen bushels of white men,
but none with a soul heavy as an anvil,
like this Sprockett, a face bear-ruined:
a miracle of Jesus, or Satan, he lived,
with the help of a Pawnee.

"He faded into the night right before
we raided Lawrence," Sprockett confessed.
"The memory of what we done there
will haint my sleep forever. Worse,
that wolf-rage keeps gnawing at my gut."

"You don't deserve to sleep," I shot back,
not one to keep quiet, even when Missus
tried to lay a bullwhip on me after her husband
and son were killed in the War: her man
bad as her, though he never tried to poke me.

"You were born," he joked, buzzard-cruel,
"ugly as a rat bred to a porcupine, unlike
Ophelia, here," and he'd grab her titties
while she flinched through her smile.
"She turns heads clear to Little Rock,"
no secret where he spent nights.

After him and his boy were killed,
Missus took a whip to her, for revenge.

"Leave off!" I spat, Missus cracking
that leather snake at me, but I grabbed
that rawhide water moccasin
and smacked her with it, then tied her up,

so if she tried to squirm out,
it'd cut her like a ham, then shoved a rag
down her throat to shut her up, and took
what I was owed from her strongbox.

Last, I strapped my skillet to my back
and ambled out, heading west, into the world.

John Sprockett Tries to Explain Why He Participated in the Raid on Lawrence

I was all riled like a bee-stung hound.
at what the Captain swore was done
to our Secesh women in that Kansas City
jail that blew like a mountain top,
Captain oathing Yankees had set the fire,
though I knew there was more to the story
than he let on; still, I frothed for revenge.

Besides, I knew the fellers riding on Lawrence,
and even if they didn't treat me so good
when we were kids, they were as close
to family as I had left: Ma and Neddy dead.

So I threw in with them, knowing our raid
would get bloody as the Red Sea,
but I thought I could ride through Lawrence,
firing into the air. But when we descended
on that farm east of town, I shot the farmer
and his son, and once we hit Lawrence,
it was blasting targets at a county fair
to win your sweet gal some prize or other,

'til I reloaded, and saw the bodies,
all those bodies upon bodies in the street.

It pains me I took part, pains me
to know I'll go wolf-wild again,
though never knowing when,
so best for everyone if I keep riding
into the mountains, always a need
for pelts, and if you accompany me,

Miz Williams, if only part of the way,
you might smooth down the rage
that roars out of me, like that grizzly
that tried to scrape off my face
and feast on the rest of me.

Sylvia Williams, after John Sprockett Has Told His Story

Him telling me what he done
in Lawrence was him asking me
to save his soul, what white folks
regularly require of us, like saying
we got to love them though
they keep us in chains and whipped.

"Last night," he sighs,
"when we camped, you kept
the fantods off me," his way of
thanking me for holding his hand
while he trembled and screamed
to wake himself, and also his way
of asking me to ride west with him.

His hand shook when he poured coffee
onto the morning embers of our campfire:
fingers still remembering the bodies
his guns had piled like cordwood,
when him and the other Secesh devils
blasted that minding-its-own-business-
Abolitionist town where I might've settled.

When I skedaddled from that plantation
and its whip-slashing white-bitch missus,
I'd no way to cypher how far it was
to the Colorado gold fields, but I'd heard
that a woman with a skillet and recipes
could make her fortune there.

"First," I warned, "try anything funny
with your pale pecker, I'll carve you
like a turkey. Second," I demanded,
"Do you know how to read and write?"
He nodded. "Then you'll teach me."

"We'll start tonight," he said,
relieved, and nudged his roan
into a meringue-smooth canter.

John Sprockett Begins to Teach Sylvia Williams How to Read and Write

I've never taught anyone before,
and never a runaway slave
who makes me mind my manners.
So I take out the book of poems
Ma was always reading to me from,
and recite a few by Mr. Shakespeare,
just to get us started.

But Miz Williams squnches up her nose
at the old-fashioned words I'm partial to,
even if I'm a Hell-bound killer.

I point at the letters, tell what each is,
have her scratch them in the dirt
with a stick; then make her say them,
not knowing if I'm going about it
in the right, school-teacher way,
and all of a sudden it's full dark.

"Recite one of them poems again,"
she asks; I pick the one that says
the woman he loves is a summer day.
When I stop, she says goodnight.

She's warned me not to try anything funny,
and though she's homely as a knothole,
and that might make some fellas
tell themselves they'd done her a favor,
Ma raised me never to take liberties.

I'm a monster to most, but she's fearless,
and teaching her gives us something
to make the miles west go faster.

John Sprockett Helps Buy a Mount for Sylvia Williams: September 1863

We've ridden one tired mount through Kansas,
and at a plains town's livery stable, the owner,
shotgun to hand, stares at my bear-slashed face,
knowing me for one of Quantrill's devils
that massacred Lawrence,
before my conscience mauled me,
but cleaner than that bear done.

"I know who you are," his voice shakes.
"Keep riding."

"First, this fine lady needs a mount."
He weighs if he can refuse on account
of her color, or maybe put one over on us,
when she points to a gun-gray mare.

"Ain't for sale," he spits tobacco. I let him
take a good long look at the scars
that talon my face, and for him to understand
we ain't moving without that mare.

I toss a coin and demand a bill of sale.
Miz Williams sits her like a Comanche
born to ride without a saddle.

"I'll call her Miz Shakespeare," she laughs,
"for all the poems you been teaching me."
For the first time in our riding together,
a smile warms my face like daybreak,
like that summer day the Bard wrote about.

Then she digs into a pouch she keeps tied
around her neck and to my surprise, repays me.

"I was a tad more enterprising than I've let on,"
she allows, all the hint I need to know,
or at least suspect, she lightened her mistress'
fortune by a bit before Miz Williams took her leave.

Sylvia Williams Saves John Sprockett from Hanging

Soon as we rode into this Jayhawker town—
where, if I'd been alone, I'd've been tolerated—
folks glared at John's bear-ripped face that hollered,
"I'm the Secesh slaughterer of Lawrence, Kansas!
What do you Abolitionist devils plan to do about it?"
They surrounded our mounts: pitchforks, nooses,
sidearms, muskets, and fists at the ready.

"You can go," the feller in charge pointed at me.
"You," he spat at John, "are going to Hell right quick."
I grabbed Sprockett's Spencer rifle out of its scabbard
and leveled it at the lynch mob: that repeater
giving me more courage than I felt:

"This gun can spit rounds faster than a rattler,"
I shouted, and a path parted like for the Israelites
striding through the suddenly dry Red Sea.
We rode from town peaceful as a Quarters' Sunday:
Master too hung over to stick his root where none
of us women, house servants or field hands both, wanted it,
Mistress in church, our backs safe from her bullwhip.

That town behind us, John smiled best he can,
what with his face looking like he shaves with a saw.

"You do know I ran out of shells?" he half chuckled.

"They didn't know that," I shot back, my fingers trembling.

"'The valiant taste of death but once,'" he recited,
taking back his Spencer from my rickety fingers.

"Your friend, the Bard?" I asked. Strange,
that a man who kills without blinking can spout poetry
by the hour; hell, by the day, whilst we ride together.

Ellis Townshend, Mayor of Chatham

Why a runaway slave woman
would ride with that Secesh murderer,
John Sprockett, I couldn't figure.
And why she'd defend him against us
that wanted to exalt him all legal,
to avenge the good, slave-hating citizens
of Lawrence, an even bigger mystery.

Them two should've been more natural
enemies than coyotes and sheep dogs,
but they seemed cozy as broke-in boots.
Wouldn't surprise me if they weren't more
than traveling companions: evenly matched
in looks, or lack of them: her squat, bow-legged,
and her face more wrinkled than a windfall
apple that's sat on the ground all winter.

And him, well, the less said about Sprockett's
bear-torn face, the better, lest I give myself
fantod nightmares the rest of my life.
I guess it's only natural them two
found each other. Who else would?

Well, good riddance. Let another town
fit a rope 'round Sprockett's neck
and welcome her with arms wide.
We may not abide slavery, but that don't
mean we'd let runaways live here,
drawing others, and before you can say,
"Abraham Lincoln," they'd have overrun
our peaceful town like jackrabbits and packrats.

Sure, everyone should live free and vote
and make a decent living. Just not here.

John Sprockett Has a Nightmare

Death hangs from me like uncleaned pelts,
even in my sleep, when all the men
I've killed descend like war-party Kiowa.

My dreams stab me like Comanche daggers,
like now, when I shoot up like a corpse
suddenly speechifying from its open coffin,

and go for my blade to fight off an attack.
But there's only Miz Williams.
Anyone else would've run like all of Hell's

after them, when I bellow and swing
my knife arm like a harvest scythe,
but she grabs my hand, and soothes me

like a colt spooked by thunder and lightning,
and somehow gets the Bowie blade away
before I can kill her or myself, with it.

She holds me, strokes my hair, even the side
of my face that grizzly's claws marked.
Finally, my breathing's not a spavined nag

laboring up a mountain, and I've forgotten
the faces I've sent to the next world
before they were ready to leave this one.

Well, not so much forgotten, as able
to put them in a room with a closed door,
but I can't ever get it to stay locked.

At the Town of Quarry, Colorado Territory, Sylvia Williams Parts Company with John Sprockett

I stare into John's grizzly-ruined face:
"This is where I stop, this town of folks
that look like me, now that we're sitting
in the crotch of the Rockies,"
where John will hide from what that bear
done to him and from what he's capable of.
"This town'll do me fine, to open a restaurant,"
I point to an empty store front.

He nods, and I'm 'bout to cry, something
I never did in all my years of slavery,
but missing his company already.
How can I ever repay him for teaching me
to read and write, for forcing that stable owner
to sell me this fine mount, when the no-good
cracker sneered he didn't treat with slaves,
even freed ones, and John just stared,
'til that giant gob of gall wet himself?

Now there's a sign saying anyone who wants
to make good use of this store is welcome,
so we cross the street to the general store,
for a Dutch oven, utensils, and tin plates.

The feller behind the counter tries
not to stare at John, hell, at us, while he smiles
a welcome to me, and shifts foot to foot,
like he'll piss himself: John's reputation
stampeding ahead of him, even here.
I plunk down the necessary I saved
and stole when I slaved for a mistress
who loved the heft of her bullwhip on my back.

Then we amble outside again, John's arms full.
But do I really want our time together to end?
Not for the protection of a really bad man,
but for how well we rubbed together these weeks
of riding west: sharing stories and laughter,
him reciting poems, when his devils let him be,
me cooking for him, a man who enjoyed his vittles,
neither of us wanting to spoil things with some sugar.

Well, wanting's got nothing to do with it;
it's time we parted, though I've got a feeling
this ain't the last I'll be seeing of John Sprockett.

John Sprockett Bids Farewell to Sylvia Williams

We stand by the hitching post,
our mounts nickering like old friends.

My heart's gripped by that bear,
now that we're parting company:
me a nightmare of scars and rage,
her, a funny looking little lady
with her witch-cackle and opinions
held hard as Jesus' facts:
the one person not afraid
of my face and reputation:

Killing, I've learned, is easy;
friendship with a butcher like me,
well that's a sight harder.

We must be staring at each other
for a good hour, neither of us
saying a word, neither of us
likely to, no place for me
among civilized folks,
white or Black, no place for her
in the gasping-for-air mountains
I intend to settle in alone.
Finally I find the words
we've both been avoiding.

"Goodbye, Miz Williams,"
my voice cracks.

"Goodbye, Mr. Sprockett,"
she kisses me
where that grizzly marked me
as Satan's bastard son,

then before she strides into
her new restaurant,
her new, free life, she laughs
like scratches on a washboard,

"You can call me 'Sylvie,'
you've earned the right."

About the Author

Robert Cooperman was born and raised in the less than mean and wild streets of Brooklyn, New York, playing, as a kid, stickball, street football, and basketball, all not very well, but very enthusiastically. After graduating from Brooklyn College with a B.A. and Long Island University with an M.A., in English, Cooperman headed west for the Ph.D. program in Literature and Creative Writing at the University of Denver.

After graduating, he taught for five years at the University of Georgia, all the time continuing to write. His first collection was *In the Household of Percy Bysshe Shelley,* published by the University Press of Florida. Cooperman's second publication was *In the Colorado Gold Fever Mountains* (Western Reflections), which won the Colorado Book Award for Poetry in 2000, and which also cemented Cooperman's love for all things about the Colorado Territory, especially a badman by the name of Mountain Jim Nugent, whom Cooperman renamed John Sprockett and has written extensively about his fictionalized adventures and misadventures. At one point Cooperman confided, "I've killed the son-of-a-bitch off three times, but he refuses to stay dead." So he just rolls with tales about this "saint of violence." Sprockett has appeared in four other collections: half murderous outlaw, half defender and avenger of the innocent.

In addition, Cooperman won the Holland Award from Logan Street Press for *My Shtetl,* a collection that drew upon his Jewish upbringing. *Draft Board Blues* (FutureCycle Press) was named One of Ten Great Books by a Colorado Author for 2017 by *Westword Magazine*. It details Cooperman's battle to keep from getting killed in the Vietnam War. Most recently, he has published *Reefer Madness* (Kelsay Books), half about Cooperman's misspent youth and half based on a newspaper article in the *Denver Post,* which stated that the Girl Scouts of Colorado had given approval for its member-troops to sell cookies outside Colorado marijuana dispensaries. You really can't make this stuff up. Forthcoming from Apprentice House is *Go Play Outside*, Cooperman's love song to basketball; and from FutureCycle Press, *Bearing the Body of Hector Home*.

Cooperman lives in Denver with his wife, Beth.

www.ingramcontent.com/pod-product-compliance
Lightning Source LLC
Chambersburg PA
CBHW022140160426
43197CB00009B/1363